IMOGEN CUNNINGHAM: PHOTOGRAPHS

Imogen Cunningham
PHOTOGRAPHS

With an Introduction by Margery Mann

SEATTLE & LONDON

UNIVERSITY OF WASHINGTON PRESS

Preface

Several years ago, I arrived early at the San Francisco Museum of Art to hear a lecture by Robert Frank. The museum was a whirlwind of excitement as dozens of barefoot art students skittered back and forth in complicated ballet patterns, hanging hundreds of yards of bright pink cloth and streamers to transform the dismal rotunda into an appropriate setting for a charity ball. I was soon joined by a small woman wearing an ankle-length black cape and a peace pin, with a red Indian pillbox hat, heavily embroidered and sparkling with mirrors, firmly anchored to a loose bun of long white hair. We watched together for some time in silence. A man looked at his watch and called out that the time was getting short, and the activity became even more frenzied.

The small woman turned to me in disapproval. "Such a lot of work," she said, "just so a few rich people can have a good time," and she turned on her thick rubber heel and stalked off.

I did not meet Imogen Cunningham until two years later, when I was writing a review of her retrospective show at the San Francisco Museum of Art for the magazine, *Artforum*. The editors of *Artforum* were feuding with the administration of the San Francisco Museum, and *Artforum*'s critics were greeted stonily by the public relations office. The review prints were pretty well picked over before they were offered to us, and sometimes when we asked, there were no prints left. Imogen's retrospective was an important show, and I wanted something more typical of her work than the one print that other reviewers had passed by, so I telephoned her. It was 11:30 in the morning, and she invited me to lunch. Immediately. She lives in an attractive small house with a large garden on Green Street, the only house in several blocks with a garden in front of it. I exclaimed over the five kinds of

Christmas roses blooming beside the front steps, and she was surprised and delighted that I knew what they were. We found that we were both plant lovers and that our ideas were usually in agreement about the function of the camera.

This book, then, is the result of hundreds of hours of discussion of flowers and photographs.

My thanks to George Craven for his permission to use material from *The Group f/64 Controversy, an Introduction to the Henry F. Swift Memorial Collection of the San Francisco Museum of Art*, a pamphlet written to accompany the exhibit in 1963, and for his correspondence answering my further questions; to Sam Ehrlich for comments and suggestions; and to Thomas K. Vasey for helping to edit the manuscript.

M. M.

Introduction

In America, we poke fun at certain primitive people who run away from the camera because they are afraid that the photographer will steal a piece of their souls. But they are quite right. A good portrait *does* take away a piece of a human soul, sometimes so that the photographer can carry it home to examine it more closely at his leisure; sometimes simply to preserve it; sometimes even to destroy it. But in return — and this is usually overlooked — the creative photographer leaves a piece of his own soul. Any photographer who takes the time to react to what he is photographing as well as to aim the lens and push the button at it — in contrast to the tourists on a guided bus trip as they ride through any city, clicking their cameras at the sights, recording them without seeing them — will never feel the same about his subject after he has photographed it. His contemplation will have given him a deeper understanding of whatever he has photographed, be it mountains or plants or people. And his photograph should tell how he reacted — if he was awed and excited by the magnificence of the scenery or would have been happier treading the hard city pavements; if he was fascinated by the design or botanical nature of the plants or had merely seen so many photographs of plants that he considered them one of the acceptable subjects for photography; or if he enjoyed or thoroughly disliked the person in front of his camera. Indeed, if he dislikes his subject, a devil lurking within his subconscious will prod the photographer into squeezing the shutter release when the person looks silly or unpleasant.

The good photographic portrait is a collaboration, a transaction, between photographer and sitter, just as a painted portrait is a collaboration between painter and sitter, and it reveals the personalities of both photographer and person photographed. We are here considering portraits that go beyond the mere recording of a person's existence—the photographer's six-month-old baby, for example, or the movie star who inadvertently walked in front of his lens. The photographer and his human subject are connected by a thread that is delicate and tenuous. If the two establish rapport, the photograph will be a success. The subject will feel that the photographer has had the insight to see his best qualities, and the photographer will feel that he has perceived the essential human being. Thus it is the photographer's responsibility to choose the particular fraction of a second by which the person would wish to be remembered. Portrait photography is difficult, and the establishing of contact is nerve-wracking, for the portrait sitting is often a meeting of strangers who are ill at ease with each other because they are uncomfortably aware that their meeting must, in a short time, produce a mutually satisfactory result.

The ordinary commercial portrait photographer therefore finds it easier to turn off his reactions to people and to reproduce them superficially and glossily, using standardized lighting and backgrounds to produce standardized human beings. One has only to examine the window of a successful portrait studio or, even more painful, to study the blank little faces in a high school yearbook to see that the photographer has in no way responded to his subjects. He has known nothing about them before he saw them on the ground glass, and, after he has mounted the prints, he knows nothing more. He has merely turned out the portraits as products no more individualized or important than the cans of tomatoes on the supermarket shelves. He has packaged human beings with as little emotional involvement as that of the canner who packaged the tomatoes, and for his work he will, like the canner, earn a living.

Certain other photographers cram their subjects into their own personal mold so tightly and unmercifully that the portrait is no longer an expression of the individual's personality but a photographic tour de force, a trophy of the photographer's victory over yet one more human soul. The portrait—painting or photograph—will become the record for future generations of how a famous man looked. If our imaginations turn to the painter Aubrey Beardsley, whose work is currently enjoying a return to fashion, we see him as he was photographed by Frederick Evans, although the Evans portrait is so idealized and ascetic that we cannot imagine this Beardsley making such lusty, rococo drawings.

The creative portrait photographer interprets his subject's personality through his own, and the dominance of photographer or subject in the print will depend on how they see each other as they size each other up. Mathew Brady's thirty-five portraits of Lincoln are clear evidence of his admiration. Brady stays in the background. The twentieth-century viewer is curious about Lincoln and does not ask who made the photograph. In England at about the same time, Julia Margaret Cameron, an enthusiastic amateur photographer, was all but bludgeoning her family friends, Alfred, Lord Tennyson and Sir John Herschel, into accompanying her into her glasshouse so that she might make their portraits. Tennyson seems calm and resigned, but Herschel seems all but defeated by this determined woman, and what Helmut Gernsheim describes in the Herschel portrait as "the majesty and energy of genius" might equally well be interpreted as an acute desire to be elsewhere.

The portrait photographer is, to quote Imogen Cunningham, "hung up on people." He likes and respects them. Yet he is aware of their weaknesses and faults. He loves them and he hates them. He responds to them, and they exhilarate and exhaust him. He does not need to know his subjects as friends, for he is constantly studying human foibles and folly and has become quick to assess what kind of person sits in front of his lens. But the understanding of the human soul often causes more pain than pleasure. "I have to mail people their proofs these days." Imogen Cunningham licks an envelope. "I can't stand it any more to be there when they first see themselves. So many people dislike themselves so thoroughly that they never see any reproduction of themselves that suits. None of us is born with the right face. It's a tough job being a portrait photographer."

Photography began in 1839—the year Daguerre's wonderful discovery was announced to the Académie des Sciences in Paris—and Imogen Cunningham began photographing in 1901. Thus, the medium of photography existed for sixty-two years without Imogen and has been enlivened by her contribution to it for sixty-nine years. "Some people," she says sharply, "believe I began in the wet plate days, but I never used wet plates. I never even knew anyone who used them."

In the sixty-nine years, Imogen (it seems revealing that everyone who knows her, including her students and grandchildren, calls her "Imogen") has been turning her creative camera on many things, but primarily on people and plants. Although she claimed once—in answer to Dorothea Lange who said to her, "I suppose you'll be remembered for your plant photographs"—that she had turned her camera on anything that could be exposed to light, she was not being entirely accurate. Imogen is a complete humanist, and a complete believer in the integrity of every individual human being. She has never photographed crowds of people. She has always selected one or two people and made them memorable. She has never photographed expanses of ocean or mountains or forest. She has always photographed individual plants and has given them the same concentrated attention that she has given her people. And she is an evangelical humanist. To a friend who exhibited a large collection of beautifully designed prints of walls, she offered moderate praise, "Very nice, but where are the people?"

Imogen Cunningham was born in Portland, Oregon, on April 12, 1883. Her father had moved to Portland from Texas after his first wife died, and since he had three small children, he wrote to a woman he knew in Missouri, a widow with a child, and invited her to come west to marry him. Imogen comments that there was nothing unusual in that kind of proposal. A widow without money was lucky to get the opportunity to have a new husband and home. Imogen was the first child of six born of her father's second marriage. Her father was a grocery clerk for a short time in Portland, then turned to farming. When he heard of a communal farm that was being established at Port Angeles, Washington, her father, who was an idealist and a believer in cooperatives, moved his family north. The communal farm was unsuccessful, and since he had to support his large family, her father moved to Seattle in 1889 where he operated street-grading equipment for a while, then went into the wood and coal business.

In 1901, when she was in high school in Seattle, Imogen saw reproductions of Gertrude Käsebier's photographs, among them the classic "Blessed Art Thou among Women," and was so enchanted with them that she decided to become a photographer herself, only hoping that her work would some day be as splendid as Käsebier's. Her father, who, she says, never encouraged her but never put anything in her way either, built her a darkroom in the woodshed, and she sent fifteen dollars to the International Correspondence School in Scranton, Pennsylvania, for a 4 x 5 camera, a course of instructions, and a box in which the glass plates were to be returned to the school for criticism. And she began to photograph. She photographed her family and friends, and she photographed her surroundings. One of her earliest prints, made in 1901 and now in the George Eastman House collection, shows a misty swamp near her home. The swamp has since been filled and is now a part of the University of Washington campus.

Imogen was the only one of her father's ten children who went to college. Her father was self-educated: a freethinker, a vegetarian, a voracious reader, and a student of Peter Ouspensky and Mme Blavatsky. When he was seventy, he began to take correspondence courses in advanced mathematics from the University of California. He loved learning, and he wanted Imogen—whom he had named after Cymbeline's daughter, in his opinion the noblest woman in Shakespeare—to become a teacher. He saw no reason for her to have all that education when she was going to be "just a dirty photographer." Although she was interested in art, Imogen majored in chemistry at the University of Washington, which at that time had no art curriculum. She worked part time in the botany department making slides and spent her money on "Perry Pictures," little packets of sepia reproductions of European art masterpieces. After she graduated, she got a job in the Curtis Studio in Seattle where she learned commercial platinum printing. In 1900, Edward S. Curtis had begun the enormous project of recording the faces and customs of the vanishing tribes of Indians of the United States, and Imogen was one of a number of girls who printed his hundreds of negatives.

Platinum papers—using light-sensitive salts of platinum instead of the silver salts that are used today—were commonly used until the first World War. Platinum, which was imported from Russia, then became expensive and practically unavailable, and although platinum papers were made in small quantities until the early thirties, they were far too expensive for most photographers to use. Many types of paper were coated commercially, and the process was simple enough so that the photographer could make up his own solutions and coat whatever papers he desired. The platinum print looks very different from the silver print. There are no heavy blacks and no clear whites, but the range and richness of the middle tones is much greater than with silver. The emulsion is slow. The papers were not designed for enlarging, but only for contact printing by a strong light. Platinum paper was expensive even when it was invented in 1873. Today the cost would be astronomical.

Imogen stayed with the Curtis Studio for two years until, in 1909, she received a national Pi Beta Phi scholarship for further study. With the encouragement of her major professor at the University of Washington, she went to the Technische Hochschule in Dresden, where there was an outstanding department of photographic chemistry. It was a university, she says, with a curriculum much like that of Cal Tech or M.I.T. There she developed a method of coating printing papers, substituting cheap salts of lead for platinum. Her process was described in a German technical magazine, and the article was pirated by a British magazine.

Imogen learned to speak German, which she still speaks fluently but diffidently, and she spent all her free time in museums examining the paintings and sculpture she had previously known only through the Perry Pictures. Her hunger to see paintings was almost insatiable. The Perry Pictures had given her no idea of the size of the paintings, so she was constantly surprised. And when friends in Munich urged her to go to Oberammergau to see the Passion Play, which was presented only once every ten years, Imogen, a freethinker like her father, was horrified that they would expect her to waste her time and money to see "some peasant dressed up as Jesus Christ."

By this time, she knew that she was more interested in photographic expression than in chemistry, but she made few photographs while she was in Europe. She had no time, and she had no money. She was then using for most of her work a 5 x 7 camera, and the film was more expensive than she could afford. One of the surviving prints is a view of the fountain in Trafalgar Square which she made in 1910 with a little folding Kodak she had received as a going-away present from the other girls who worked at the Curtis Studio.

She also made a number of photographs of Professor Luter, her adviser, who told her that he would work out a mathematical problem in his mind while she studied him, and that she should photograph him when she felt that he had reached the greatest intensity of concentration. She says that she feels his idea was a good one, and that even today, when people are nervous about being photographed, she asks them to think about the nicest thing they know. If they aren't thinking at all, it is impossible to get a good likeness.

When she returned to Seattle, she opened a portrait studio, and it was at this period that the amalgam of realism and romanticism that is still the Cunningham style was developed. Although she was immediately successful commercially—from the day she opened her studio, she had almost all the work she could do—she still had time to read poetry with her friends, "high-flown, ethereal stuff," and to make photographs that reflected their reading. They were all admirers of William Morris, and she photographed a young painter who occupied the adjoining studio and his girl friend in all manner of dreamlike tableaux.

One of her romantic, storytelling prints, "Eve Repentant," two nudes, a contrite Eve laying her hand on Adam's shoulder begging forgiveness as he turns away, was published in a local magazine, the *Town Crier*. Although today it seems one of the least erotic photographs of the twentieth century, it was a sensation in Seattle in 1910. This was a puritan era. Only two years later, Anthony Comstock, secretary of the Society for the Suppression of Vice, saw Paul Chabas' gentle, undistinguished painting, "September Morn," in the window of a gallery on 46th Street in New York and damned it so violently that the painting was reproduced on calendars for twenty years. "Eve Repentant" was not so fortunate. The controversy was confined to angry letters in the local newspaper, but the scandal was explosive in Seattle, which Imogen describes at that time as "Boston moved west."

Her commercial portraiture in 1910 is typified by the elegant "Mrs. Elizabeth Champney." Mrs. Champney, who lived in a nearby hotel, was the author of *Vassar Girls Abroad* as well as a number of flamboyant histories: *Romance of Imperial Rome, Romance of Old Belgium from Caesar to Kaiser, Romance of Old Japan, Romance of Russia from Rurik to Bolshevik.* This was Imogen's first commission when she opened her studio. The portrait embodies a carefully designed, straightforward seeing completely at odds with the romantic fantasies Imogen created in her spare time—although she admits that she had a book of prints of Utamaro heads, and that she pored over them earnestly just before her sitters came to her studio, hoping that the Utamaro touch would rub off.

In 1915 Imogen married the young, Paris-trained etcher, Roi Partridge, and for a couple of years they worked in adjoining studios. Their son, Gryffyd, was born two years later, and in 1917 Roi moved to San Francisco, followed by Imogen, who was very pregnant with what the doctor had predicted would be a big girl. The big girl turned out to be twin sons, Rondall and Padraic. In 1920 Roi began teaching at Mills College, and he and Imogen moved to Oakland to a house near the college campus. For several years she devoted herself to her children, to her faculty wife activities, and to helping Roi plan and hang exhibits in the college art gallery. She did some professional work, portraits of the Mills girls and publicity photographs for the Böhm Ballet, but most of her work was done for her own pleasure. She did, however, keep in contact with her photographer friends, for example, Edward Weston, whom she had met in Glendale in 1923, and, with them, she founded a photographic movement that changed the direction of West Coast photography.

Every generation of photographers, it seems, must organize to fight for the acceptance of photography as an art form. The Photo-Secession was formed for this purpose by Alfred Stieglitz in New York in 1902. There were ultimately over a hundred hand-picked members, among them Stieglitz, Clarence H. White, Edward Steichen, and Gertrude Käsebier. Their prints were usually completely romantic and painterly. A soft-focus lens made the world a hazy, idealized place appropriate to its inhabitants, costumed figures who might have escaped from the canvases of the pre-Raphaelite painters.

The Photo-Secession had only two members from the West Coast, Annie Brigman from Oakland and Oscar Maurer from San Francisco, but the influence lay heavy on photographers everywhere. The technique and the spirit of Imogen's poetic, neo-Arthurian prints made in 1910 to 1912 were the result of the common conceit that, to make the photograph "Art," the camera should remove the subject from the ordinary workaday world and carry it to a high, unearthly plane. When viewed historically as an expression of a world much less sophisticated than our own, many of the early Photo-Secession-influenced prints are charming and imaginative. The romantic sentimentality is well suited to the double portrait of Edward Weston and Margrethe Mather which Imogen made in 1923. The same year, Weston made an equally poetic and otherworldly portrait of Imogen. Only one print of this is known to exist, a platinum print on loan to the Oakland Museum. The photographers of this school called themselves "Pictorialists," but the photographs of the pictorial school ultimately degenerated into a portrayal of a sterile meaningless world, seen through a veil of photographic manipulation. Today, we use "pictorial" as a derogatory term for the monotonous prints of the camera club salons.

The reaction against the use of the camera as a painter's tool was not an influential movement in the West until the early 1930's, but it began in New York before 1920. Some of Alfred Stieglitz' prints made in the early twenties—the portrait of Georgia Engelhard made in 1921 and "Side of Barn, Lake George," about 1923, are direct and unromanticized. Charles Sheeler's most famous print, "Bucks County Barn," was made in 1915, and Sheeler, who is better remembered as a painter, photographed as straightforward a world as he painted. And Paul Strand, to whom Stieglitz devoted the last two issues of his magazine, *Camera Work*, in 1916, was already photographing the people and streets of New York with uncompromising realism. West Coast photographers continued to obscure the world to make "artistic" prints.

According to Imogen, it was Margrethe Mather, who was then Edward Weston's partner in a studio in Glendale, who encouraged Weston to use his camera as a direct window to the real world. Certainly, his work after the early twenties is no longer in the furry, soft-focus tradition of his earlier work, for example, the well-known portrait of the dancer, Ruth St. Denis, made in 1916. In the twenties, Imogen also rejected romanticism. The vision of the "Pflanzenformen" series is clear and unaffected, and the design is so contemporary that when six of the prints were used by West Coast Airlines for their 1967 calendar, it was hard to believe that the prints were forty years old.

In 1930 Ansel Adams met Paul Strand and saw his prints, and Strand's work so impressed him that thereafter he showed the mountains of the Sierra Nevada in straight, unromanticized prints. Adams, Weston, and Imogen were living near San Francisco, and they—with their friends, John Paul Edwards, Sonia Noskowiak, Willard Van Dyke, and Henry F. Swift—became the f/64 Group. Swift was the only nonprofessional. He was a stockbroker who was an amateur photographer, and he was the only member of the group with enough money to collect his friends' prints. His fairly extensive collection is housed in the San Francisco Museum of Art.

Histories of photography refer to the f/64 Group as an organized reform movement. It was not. It was a casual, informal group of friends who met together from time to time in a photography gallery that Willard Van Dyke and Mary Jeannette Edwards opened at 683 Brockhurst Street in Oakland, Annie Brigman's old studio. They met to talk about photography and to show their prints to each other and to the public. In the fall of 1932, Ansel Adams and Willard Van Dyke proposed that they become better organized to implement the spread of their ideas, and Van Dyke suggested the name. "f/64" was chosen because the members of the group were dedicated to the honest, sharply defined image, and the lens opening, f/64, provides the ultimate in resolution and depth of field. Adams felt that the membership should be limited to "those workers who are striving to define photography as an art form by a simple and direct presentation through purely photographic methods." Imogen remembers that the adoption of the name and the criterion for membership did nothing to formalize the group. "There were no officers, no regular meetings, no dues."

The f/64 Group sponsored one exhibit. It opened at the M. H. de Young Memorial Museum in San Francisco on November 15, 1932, with sixty-four prints by the members and sixteen by sympathetic nonmembers, Alma Lavenson, Consuelo Kanaga, Preston Holder, and Edward Weston's son, Brett. The impact of the new seeing was not immediate, although the show aroused considerable interest, and the critics came away from the gallery with some of their ideas about the nature of photography badly shaken. In 1933 Adams opened a gallery on Geary Street in San Francisco to show prints that exemplified the new seeing, and, with the help of his friends, Van Dyke continued to show prints at the Brockhurst Gallery.

By the spring of 1934, the organized amateur pictorialists on the West Coast considered the f/64 Group enough of a threat to their own way of seeing and their domination of the medium so that William Mortensen, the leading spokesman for the pictorialists, and one of the most skillful and enthusiastic manipulators of an original image, wrote an angry denunciation of the group in *Camera Craft*. Adams and Van Dyke equally angrily replied, and the controversy filled the pages of *Camera Craft* for almost a year and a half.

Mortensen's photographs, and the prints of his hundreds of followers, used the original negative as the merest point of departure for the final print. The negative might be retouched with knife or pencil. It was sometimes printed with the enlarging easel tilted to elongate and distort the image. It was often printed through a texture screen. The subjects were always exotic, often grotesque. Imogen recalls that a student in her class at the California School of Fine Arts once asked her opinion of Mortensen, and she refused to say what she thought but described her favorite photograph, a gorilla dragging a half-naked woman over a hilltop. It was called "L'Amour."

The f/64 photographers differed widely in technique and point of view, but their seeing was always an honest portrayal of the real world, and technique was subordinate to vision. Technique was simply the means of conveying to the printing paper what the photographer had seen so that someone else might see it too. Most of the members were using large cameras. Edward Weston used an 8 x 10 view camera, composed on the ground glass, and contact printed every negative to the edges, contending that the final print must be previsualized by the photographer, and that the creative process was over at the instant of pressing the shutter release. Peter Stackpole, a young photographer who was a frequent visitor to the Brockhurst Gallery and was much influenced by the f/64 Group although he was not a member, carried a miniature camera to the towers of the San Francisco–Oakland Bay Bridge to document the construction. Stackpole later became one of *Life's* first photographers.

The f/64 Group disbanded in 1935. Edward and Brett Weston had left the area to open a studio in Santa Monica. Adams and Van Dyke closed their galleries, and Van Dyke went to New York to make films. Imogen suggested then that they all make photographs of each other, but she says that she was too unsure of herself to press the idea, and that no one else was interested. She was not aware that the group would one day be considered a turning point in West Coast photographic vision. She just thought it might be amusing for the members one day to recall themselves as their friends had seen them in 1935.

There are probably many reasons that the seeing of the f/64 Group triumphed over pictorialism. The f/64 Group existed during the Depression, and the hard reality of the real world made the sweet romanticism of the pictorialists ridiculous. Only by facing the world squarely could one hope to survive. Those who turned aside were defeated. Photojournalism became important. It was hardly a new idea—Roger Fenton had photographed the Crimean War in 1853—but *Life* was founded in 1936, and the large-circulation photojournalism magazines gave a curious public glimpses of many exotic facets of the world that had hitherto been concealed from them, some of them as close as next door, and a public being offered such tidbits would be impatient if they were obscured by a haze.

At this time, Imogen's work was often similar to Edward Weston's both in clarity of seeing and in technique, but it was in no way imitative. The angular, highly stylized nude called "Triangles," 1928, was, in fact, made in Weston's studio, but the complex design of "Triangles" is so dominant that the nude is depersonalized. With Weston's nudes, one is always aware of the woman. Imogen was using a large camera then, and she was usually printing the full negative. But she has always been too independent a thinker to set up rules for herself and abide by them. In 1929 she was making some of the purest of her plant portraits, but she was also making a negative image of a snake that her children had brought home to her in a bucket. Today negative prints are one of the commonest clichés of "experimentation," and they are as old as Fox Talbot's photogenic drawings of 1839, but in 1929 they were far from common. Imogen had never seen one when she reversed the snake.

She has never jumped on bandwagons. She deplores today's fad for high contrast and golf-ball grain, but in spite of being one of the pioneers in the straight approach, she has not felt inhibited when she wanted to play with the medium. In 1955 she made a self-portrait with her grandchildren in a distorting mirror in a funhouse. In 1961 she photographed Man Ray in Paris, and in her darkroom in San Francisco she made a multiple print which she called "A Man Ray Version of Man Ray"—half a dozen images are superimposed to make a tall head studded with eyes—but the idea intrigued her for only one morning, and she made only one print of it.

She has been particularly fascinated by double images, and they recur in several forms in her work. The double image may be a subtle balancing of masses, of two design elements. They may be two human beings, like the two engrossed women having "Tea at Foster's" in 1950, or the photograph of John Roeder with his statue, 1961; or they may be two plant forms, like the "Two Callas," 1929, or the symmetrical trees in the "Cemetery in France," 1961. She has sometimes made two exposures on one negative. The portrait of the painter, Joseph Sheridan, made in 1929, was her earliest double exposure, and her concentration on the pattern—the repetition of the stripes of sweater, cigarettes, chair, and fence—almost obscures the man. Her finest double exposure on the negative is certainly the portrait of the poet and filmmaker, James Broughton, "The Poet and His Alter Ego," made in 1962. As Imogen moved the camera, Broughton turned his eyes. "I moved the camera a tiny bit, and I must say luck was with me, because his eyes are looking at each other, and that was *just chance*. I didn't give him any directions at all. There wasn't time for that, and it's just funny." One can only retort that "chance" is frequently kind to a sensitive photographer with sixty years' experience. She has used reflections—the "Double Image" of the woman waiting at a bus stop, 1950—and she has occasionally printed two negatives superimposed, for example, the strong but ambiguous "Mendocino Motif," 1959, and the mystic "Dream Walking," 1968.

For several years, everywhere she looked there was a real-life double image. Her twin sons left their mark on her work.

It is ironic to realize that her already classic plant photographs of the "Pflanzenformen" series, so-called because they were first exhibited in "Film und Foto" in Stuttgart in 1929, can be blamed on her children. They were made as the sublimation of her photographic drive by the mother of three small boys, so predictably mischievous that the Mills College community referred to them as "The Little Partridge Devils." In the early 1920's, when because of the children she was unable to spend much time making portraits, she became interested in plants and turned the hill behind her house into a rock garden, where she specialized in what she called "cacti." A botanist friend pointed out to her that most of her plants were not cacti but succulents, and Imogen decided to learn more about plants. She learned through study and through photographing their forms. Today she is still an enthusiastic gardener and is a member of the California Horticultural Society.

The "Magnolia Blossom" of 1925 is her most famous plant photograph—"Some people think I never did another flower"—and was one of her earliest. The magnolia, as well as some of the later plant photographs, like "Hen and Chickens," 1929, and the filmy exploding "Auragia," 1953, are studies in pure design. But most of her plant photographs are as much portraits as are her portraits of human beings. She has arranged them and considered their personalities as thoughtfully as she has her human subjects. "Amaryllis," 1933, looks very much like her portrait of Marian Simpson, a Berkeley painter, made the following year.

Imogen's interchange with her subjects is so relaxed that her portraits are perhaps less appreciated than they should be. "People are a bunch of nuts," she says, obviously including herself, "but some are nuttier than others." Since 1910, she had exhibited widely in galleries in the United States and Europe—plants, designs, a few portraits—but her portraits were seen primarily by the friends and families of her subjects. She spent the summer of 1931 in Santa Barbara where she met Martha Graham, who was there visiting her mother, and she made a number of photographs of Graham posing against the open door of her mother's old barn, the black interior contrasting starkly with the sunlit figure. Imogen knew her photographs were good, and she sent a number of prints to the editor of *Vanity Fair*, which was then the leading magazine of society, opinion, and the arts in America. The magazine bought two of them, and thereafter she worked on occasional assignments until *Vanity Fair* was absorbed by *Vogue* in 1936.

She recalls that the editor in New York had no idea that San Francisco was four hundred miles from Los Angeles and sent her to Hollywood as casually as if she had merely to cross the street. At the time, she was using a heavy, cumbersome 8 x 10 camera, and the day-long trips between Oakland and Los Angeles were tedious. In 1945 she bought a Rolleiflex, and she now has three of them. She shudders as she remembers the discomfort of carrying around her 8 x 10.

Edward Steichen was then *Vanity Fair*'s top photographer, and his studio portraits of people from the stage (Alla Nazimova, George M. Cohan, and the masterful "Paul Robeson as 'The Emperor Jones'") and from politics (Franklin D. Roosevelt, Cordell Hull, Ruth Bryan Owen) made his subjects remote, glamorous inhabitants of a higher world. Imogen, on the other hand, turned the glamorous inhabitants of the higher world into human beings.

She photographed James Cagney ("such a nice, red-haired kid, he reminded me of my own boys"); Cary Grant in the alley behind the little apartment house where he lived; Joan Blondell ("She had on a lot of those fake eyelashes, and I made her take them off, and you know, she'd worn the fake ones so long, she didn't have any of her own at all—I was an awful purist in those days"). She photographed Wallace Beery at the Burbank Airport right after he landed his Bellanca. He was wearing dirty flannel slacks, a grease-stained leather jacket, an enormous, flashing diamond ring, and his old patent leather evening pumps. "He had a terrible toothache, but he was very obliging." She photographed Upton Sinclair, who was campaigning for governor of California on the EPIC ("End Poverty in California") platform, the day before the general strike in 1934. He came into his hotel room so tired from a day of speaking that he collapsed on the bed to rest while she set up her camera. She photographed Herbert Hoover— he preferred a print where he was holding the collar of his big German shepherd dog—but he was being booed on the streets of San Francisco, and he was so controversial a figure that *Vanity Fair* decided against publishing him.

In the mid-thirties, Imogen and Roi were divorced. She continued living in Oakland until 1947 when she moved to her present house in San Francisco. She has made her living as a portrait photographer, and she has also photographed people for fun. She has had a particular affinity with painters, writers, and other photographers, and her best portraits are usually those of creative people. Even Mrs. Champney, it should be remembered, was a prolific, though florid, writer.

In 1934 Imogen photographed Alfred Stieglitz at An American Place. She had seen him in New York in 1910 on her way back from Germany when he had the 291 Gallery, but she was terrified of him then and merely walked around the gallery. In 1934, knowing that he had an 8 x 10 camera, she loaded her own 8 x 10 film holders before she went to An American Place and photographed him with his own camera. "It was a shaky old thing with a Goerz Dagor lens on it that was so oxidized that you couldn't tell the readings on the diaphragm. You couldn't tell what you were doing, and the shutter was released with one of those big hoses and a bulb, and although I began early, I had no practice with that kind of thing. So he practiced me. He really did. He practiced me making the exposure and how long it would be, and I had no meter, and I just held it as long as I could, and I put the opening where I could barely see to focus, which was probably f/11, and they were all in focus. I took seven shots and quit. This is the best one, I think, it has that grim little look in the eye, you know, disliking everything and everybody."

Her photograph of Mme Ozenfant, whom Imogen describes as a "nice little French housewife," is, atypically, more interesting than the photograph of her husband, the painter and critic, Amédée Ozenfant. The point of light emphasizes Mme Ozenfant's angular features and makes her look strong, until one sees that she is tightly holding her husband's hand. Gertrude Stein stares at us sphinxlike; Alice B. Toklas was fluttering in the background. Morris Graves is Imogen's most famous portrait. It has been widely exhibited and is in the collections of all the major museums. Minor White gave the portrait to one of his classes and asked the students to analyze it. "He had it on the cover of *aperture*, and he sent me all the class had written, and he left wide margins on the copy he sent me, and I wrote my comments on the student comments. I had no idea he was going to publish the whole thing, but my chief comment was, 'You have more philosophers than photographers.'" The portrait was made in 1950 and is considered one of the finest photographs in the history of the medium.

Many portraits of Ansel Adams are exhibited. Most of them are made by his students, and they tend to be serious and humble. Imogen's joyous portrait of Ansel on a mountaintop—once referred to by an irreverent student as "Ansel getting the word from God"—is closer to the joy in nature that Ansel's photographs communicate. Her photograph of Anna Freud was made for a group of psychiatrists who were taking full advantage of every minute that Anna Freud was in San Francisco, and allowed Imogen fifteen minutes to photograph her. If Anna Freud looks alert, it is because Imogen had just told her that she thought that most of psychoanalysis was nonsense. The tapestry designer, Mark Adams, and his wife, the printmaker Beth Van Hoesen, share a private joke as they fill an open space in one of Adams' tapestries. It is one of Imogen's most charming portraits.

The photographer who truly responds to human beings, to the whole person and not just the surface, will make even the unknown person memorable. Certainly, more people will be interested in the portrait of Gertrude Stein than will study "Rebecca," 1934, who worked for friends of Imogen's in Virginia. But Rebecca was a strong, dignified woman, and Imogen thus portrayed her. In 1960 she was driving with a friend through Germany and stopped to photograph "People on the Road." "They told us they had been to a funeral, and they were perfectly dressed for it. They seemed pretty cheerful, though, and of course he had his consolation with him in that bottle."

What Imogen calls her "documentary work" is closer to portraiture than to true social document. Social document usually makes the person a symbol rather than an individual, and Imogen cannot forget the essential humanity of each particular person. The grimacing women of the "Rummage Sale," 1948; the gentle "Sunbonnet Woman," 1950; even the anonymous woman lying on the "Bench in the Marina," 1954—Imogen has speculated about all of them. Where do they live? Who are their families? She has been trying for several years to get in touch with the beautiful girl in the "Coffee Gallery," 1960. "They called her 'Linda Lovely,' not her real name, of course, and I've asked a lot of people to have her call me. She still lives here and has a lot of little children, I've heard. She was published in an English annual, and I've been saving a copy for her."

At eighty-six, Imogen continues working. She does not accept as many portrait commissions as she did when she was younger, but since many private and government collections are buying her prints—the Exchange National Bank in Chicago and the Smithsonian Institution have recently bought a number of them—she usually spends her mornings in the darkroom. Her work is in George Eastman House, the Museum of Modern Art, and the Oakland Museum. Several years ago, the Library of Congress bought a collection of her prints. "They wanted famous people, and I sold them forty of them—five dollars a head."

Within the last few years, most of the major museums in northern California have given her retrospective exhibits, and, although she has a large supply of old negatives to draw from, every show contains a few new prints. In northern California this is almost unheard of, for many photographers continue to give show after show of fifteen-year-old work.

In 1961 she was interviewed for the Regional Cultural History Project of the University of California, and the transcript is on file in the Bancroft Library. The interview is a colorful, rambling account of Imogen's life and thoughts on photography. In 1964 she was made an honorary member of the American Society of Magazine Photographers, and in the same year Minor White devoted an issue of *aperture* (Volume 11, Number 4) to her work, with an essay by George Craven. *Infinity* for November, 1966, contained an appreciation of her work. She has recently appeared in two films. She starred in Fred Padula's film, "Two Photographers: Imogen Cunningham and Wynn Bullock," and she appeared twice in James Broughton's prize-winning bit of ribaldry, "The Bed." John Korty is currently making a film about her and her work. She teaches at the San Francisco Art Institute and lectures occasionally at San Francisco State College, Foothill College, and University of California Extension, and in the summer of 1968 she was in charge of an eight-week workshop at Humboldt State College in Arcata.

In 1967 Imogen and Martha Graham were the only two women to be made Fellows of the National Academy of Arts and Sciences, an interesting coincidence, since it was her prints of Martha Graham that had brought Imogen's portraits national attention. Imogen had seen Graham's farewell tour with her company in the fall of 1966 and had visited her backstage after the performance. "Oh, yes, she knew me—when she saw me outside the door, she stopped all the other people and let me come in. She's tremendously well preserved."

The California College of Arts and Crafts in Oakland conferred on her the honorary degree of Doctor of Fine Arts in May of 1968. Since she wore her conspicuous peace symbol on a chain around her neck, she was wildly cheered by the sympathetic students. Her son, Ron, refers to her affectionately as "my hippie mother."

When she was asked recently to comment on her work, Imogen shrugged her shoulders. "There's too much philosophizing about photography already these days. And the Zen people are the Most. People will just have to look at my stuff and make up their own minds." Her diffidence, her friendly informality, and her refusal to advance theories or to pontificate about her work have made her seem a much less complex person than she is. Yet her photographs, from 1910 to 1969, show such a constant antithesis between romanticism and realism that they could have been made by two people. In 1910 she photographed "The Wind," a beautiful young woman with a chiffon veil over her face, and she waited until the veil was blown against her model's face so that her features were delineated. The same year, she photographed "Mrs. Champney," a direct, straightforward portrait. In 1968 she made the haunting double image, "Dream Walking"; yet her portrait of Ruth Asawa beside the door she had carved for her house is no less sensitive but is completely literal.

Some small case might be made for the argument that her commercial work is realistic, while the work she does for her own pleasure is romantic. But the case would be hard to defend. She photographed Ruth Asawa because they are friends, and in the history of photography no more realistic photographs have been made than the plant photographs she made for herself in the thirties. Yet she has throughout her career posed her family and friends in compositions of her own imagining: "My Father at 90," 1936, sitting in front of the wood he had chopped for his winter supply; "Shen Yao," 1938, now a professor of linguistics at the University of Hawaii, with her hands clasped and an unfurled fan behind her head; Mrs. Pabst with a trailing vine to show "Age and Its Symbols," 1958; Barbara Cannon Myers with skeletonized leaves to make "The Taiwan Leaves," 1963. For almost sixty years, her work has gone in two completely opposite directions, and the dichotomy has not bothered Imogen in the least.

She has also not been particularly concerned that her championship of pure vision expressed in pure technique has not prevented her from making multiple images whenever it has suited her fancy. If a multiple image has improved the design or carried her message more adequately, she has made one. If she has taken the time to think about the discrepancy, she has thought it amusing. For she has that rarest of all qualities among photographers, a sense of humor.

Although she has been interested primarily in portraits and plants, she has made many other successful photographs. One of her nudes, photographed in 1932 and named by one of her sons "Ruthie's

Rear," was published in *U.S. Camera Annual,* and during World War II Imogen received letters from servicemen all over the world who had cut it out for a pin-up. She also received a wistful letter from a friend, a doctor stationed in the South Pacific. He had seen the photograph so many times that he thought it would enhance his prestige if he had an original print. She was happy to send him a print, but because of his medical training she felt that another print would interest him more. She sent him a nude pregnant woman.

"The Unmade Bed," one of her most popular prints, was made as a joke. If one of her photographer friends marries, she gives it as a warning to the new husband. "He should know what kind of life he'll lead." A student at the California School of Fine Arts had unhappily told Imogen of Dorothea Lange's only assignment to her class: "Make a meaningful photograph of your environment without people." In the morning Imogen looked at her rumpled sheets, arranged the hairpins, and made the photograph. She sent a contact print to Dorothea, who phoned her to ask for an enlargement and to invite her to the last meeting of the class. Her print was hung beside one of a remarkably messy desk. Imogen felt it unfair that her print should be so used unless she knew whose desk it was. "He's right behind you," said Dorothea. Imogen turned to see Dorothea's husband, Paul Taylor, a professor of economics at the University of California.

Imogen's success has in no way made her self-satisfied. "I've lived so long and stayed with photography so long that people are curious about what makes me tick. I suppose that by the time most people are my age, they have it made. Maybe it's the lack of money that pushes me along. I've always worked for money, and I've always had fun doing it. People often marvel at me. 'I don't know how you keep so busy,' they say. *Keep* busy," she repeats impatiently. "I don't *keep* busy. I *am* busy."

Her best photograph, she still feels, will be made tomorrow.

Plates

1. Marsh at Dawn, 1901

2. Trafalgar Square, 1910

3. Mrs. Elizabeth Champney, Writer, 1910

4. Eve Repentant, 1910

5. The Wind, about 1910

6. The Wood beyond the World, about 1912

7. Roi Partridge, Etcher, 1915

8. *Mills College Amphitheater, about 1920*

9. Nude, 1923

10. Edward Weston and Margrethe Mather, 1923

11. Magnolia Blossom, 1925

12. Triangles, 1928

13. Two Callas, about 1929

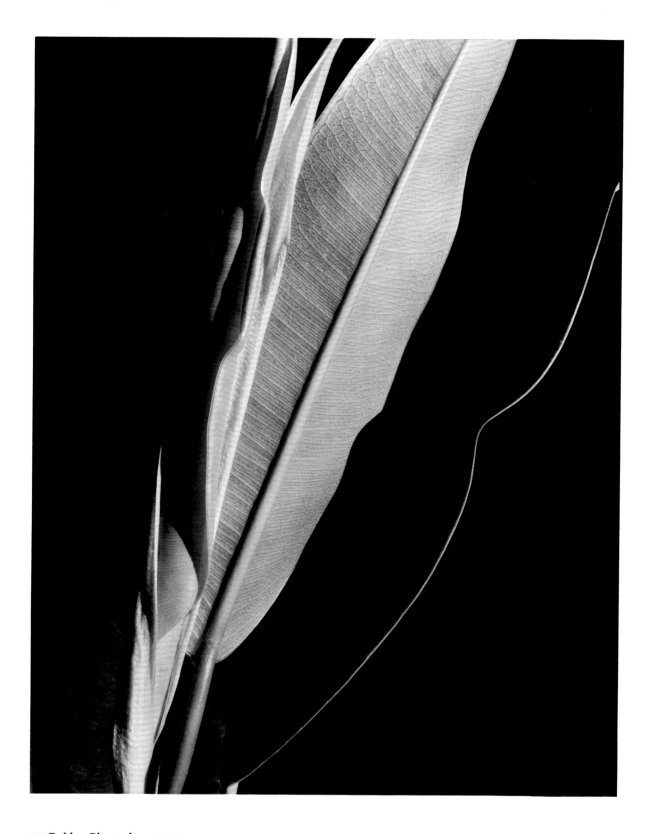

14. *Rubber Plant, about 1929*

15. Hen and Chickens, 1929

16. Joseph Sheridan, Painter, 1929

17. Snake, 1929

18. Braille, 1930

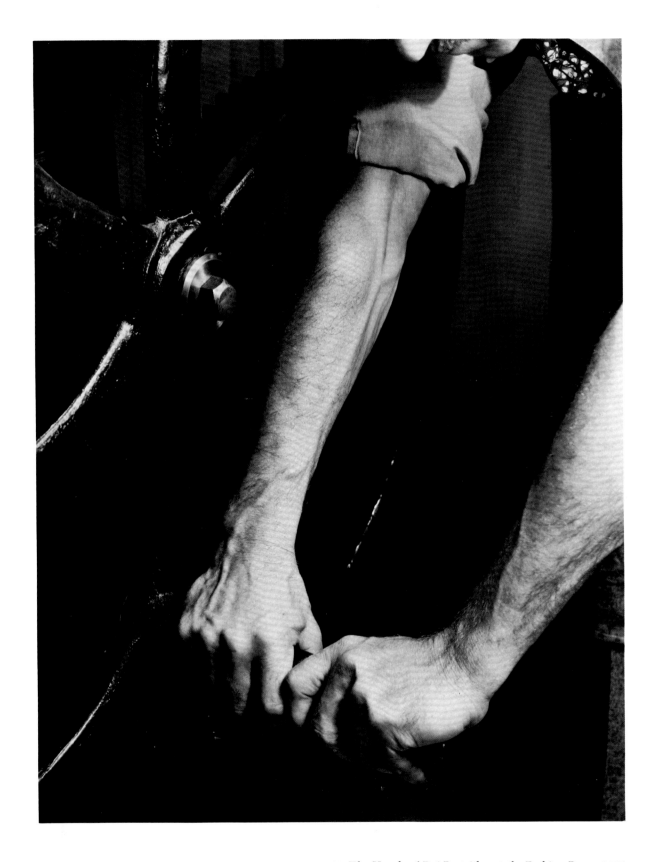

19. *The Hands of Roi Partridge at the Etching Press, 1930*

20. The Bruton Sisters, Artists, 1930

21. Martha Graham, Dancer, 1931

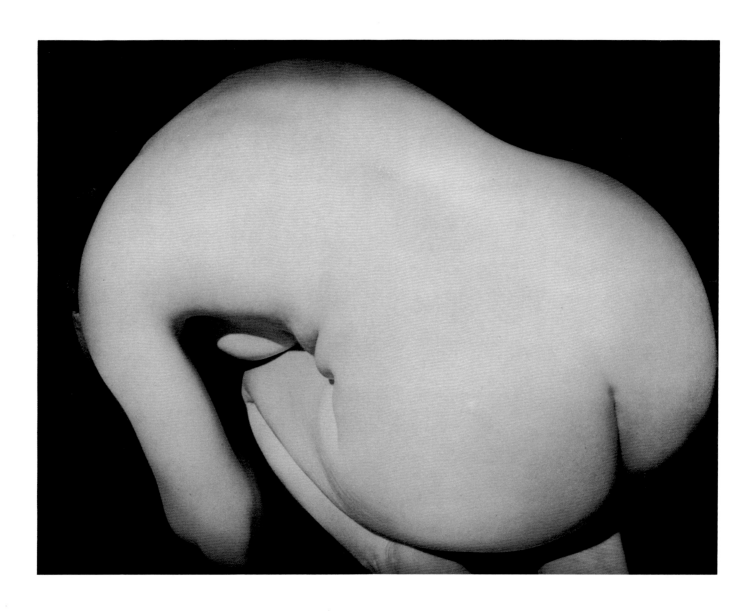

22. Nude, 1932

23. *Cary Grant, Actor, 1932*

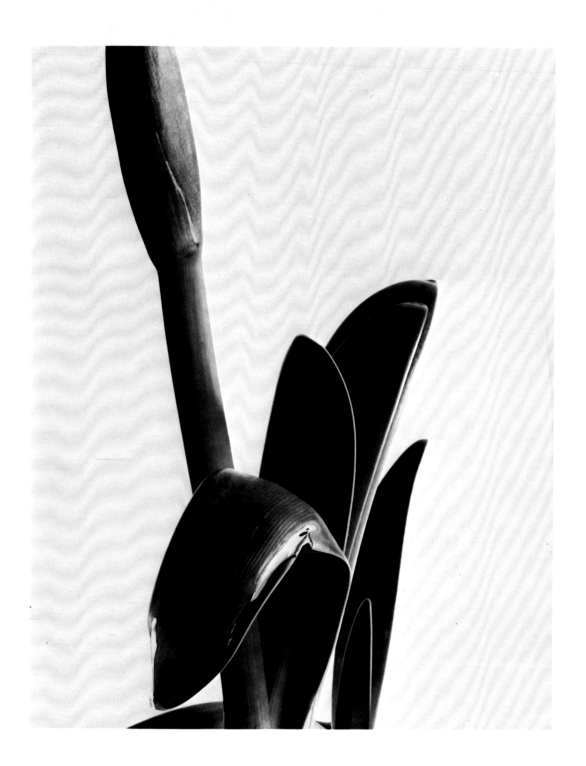

24. *Amaryllis, 1933*

25. Fageol Ventilators, 1934

26. Alfred Stieglitz, Photographer, 1934

27. Marian Simpson, Painter, 1934

28. Upton Sinclair, 1934

29. Rebecca, Hume, Virginia, 1934

30. *Amédée Ozenfant, Painter and Critic, 1935*

31. Mme Ozenfant, 1935

32. Helena Mayer, Fencer, 1935

33. My Father at Ninety, 1936

34. *Frieda Kahlo Rivera, Painter and Wife of Diego Rivera, 1937*

35. Herbert Hoover, 1937

36. Gertrude Stein, Writer, 1937

37. The Three Harps, 1937

38. *Shen Yao, Professor of Linguistics at the University of Hawaii, 1938*

39. Lyonel Feininger, Painter, 1941

40. Edward Weston, Photographer, with His Cats, 1945

41. Discrimination at a Rummage Sale, 1948

42. *Leaves, 1948*

43. Tea at Foster's, before 1950

44. *Morris Graves, Painter, 1950*

45. Double Image, about 1950

46. Sunbonnet Woman, about 1950

47. Alone, about 1950

48. Ansel Adams, Photographer, 1953

49. Auragia, 1953

50. Bench in the Marina District, San Francisco, 1954

51. Self-Portrait with Grandchildren in the Funhouse, 1955

52. Negro Boy in New York, 1956

53. Merce Cunningham, Dancer, 1957

54. The Unmade Bed, 1957

55. Ruth Asawa, Sculptor, and Her Children, 1958

56. David Park, Painter, 1958

57. Self-Portrait on Geary Street, 1958

58. *Age and Its Symbols, 1958*

59. Mendocino Motif, 1959

60. Pregnant Woman, 1959

61. Theodore Roethke, Poet, 1959

62. Stan, 1959

63. On St. Germain, Paris, 1960

64. Mark Shorer, Writer, 1960

65. Anna Freud, 1960

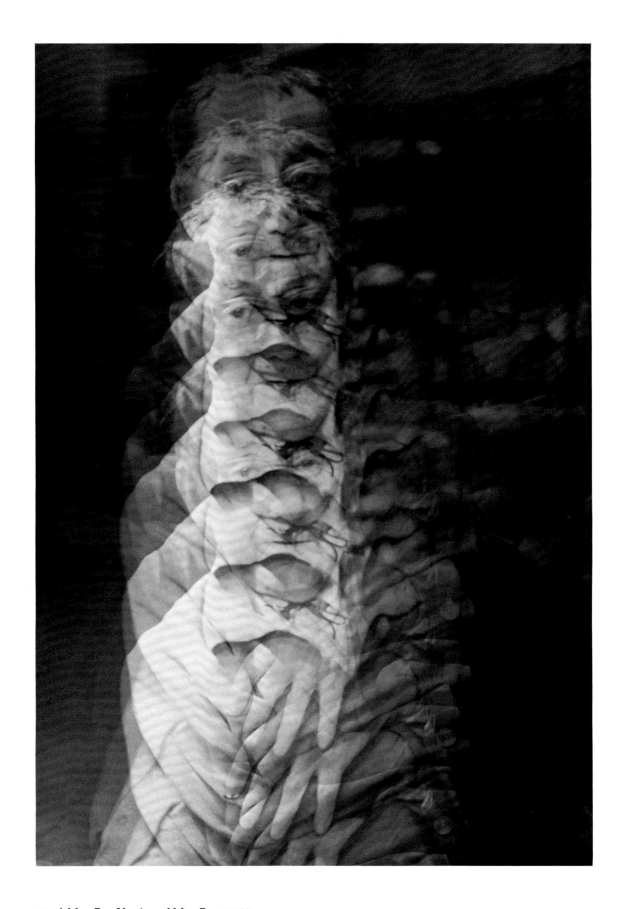

66. A Man Ray Version of Man Ray, 1960

67. Man Ray, Photographer, Paris, 1960

68. People on the Road, Germany, 1960

69. August Sander, Photographer, at Home, 1960

70. Coffee Gallery, San Francisco, 1960

71. The Savonarola Look (Barbara Cannon Myers), 1960

72. *Woman on the German Train, 1960*

73. Cemetery in France, 1961

74. *John Roeder and His Sculpture, 1961*

75. Restaurant in Chartres, 1961

76. Woman in a Polish Restaurant, 1961

77. *The Poet and His Alter Ego (James Broughton, Poet and Filmmaker), 1962*

78. The Taiwan Leaves, 1963

79. Mark Adams, Tapestry Designer, and His Wife, the Printmaker Beth Van Hoesen, 1963

80. Minor White, Photographer, 1963

81. Ruth Asawa, Sculptor, 1963

82. Crab Nets, 1963

83. Three Heads and Four Hands, 1964

84. Barbara at the Door, 1965

85. Wynn Bullock, Photographer, 1966

86. Scene from "The Bed," 1967

87. Scene from "The Bed," 1967

88. Alice-Marie on Haight Street, 1967

89. Ruth Asawa, Sculptor, 1968

90. Phoenix, 1968

91. Phoenix Recumbent, 1968

92. Dream Walking, 1968

93. Haight Street, 1968

94. Warning, 1970

Exhibitions

1912   Brooklyn Institute of Arts and Sciences, New York (one-man)

1929   "Film und Foto" at the Deutscher Werkbund, Stuttgart (group)

1932   Los Angeles County Museum (one-man)

1932   M. H. de Young Memorial Museum, San Francisco (one-man)

1932   "Group f/64" at the M. H. de Young Memorial Museum,
        San Francisco (group)

1935   Dallas Art Museum (one-man)

1936   E. B. Crocker Art Gallery, Sacramento, California (one-man)

1937   "Photography 1839–1937" at the Museum of Modern Art,
        New York (group)

1940   "A Pageant of Photography" at the Golden Gate International Exposition,
        San Francisco (group)

1951   San Francisco Museum of Art (one-man)

1953   Mills College, Oakland, California (one-man)

1954   "Perceptions" at the San Francisco Museum of Art (group)

1955   "San Francisco Weekend," Bay Area Photographers Show,
        San Francisco (group)

1956   Cincinnati Museum of Art (one-man)

1956   Limelight Gallery, New York (one-man)

1957   Oakland Art Museum, Oakland, California (one-man)

1959   Oakland Public Museum, Oakland, California (one-man)

1959   "Photography at Mid-Century" at George Eastman House,
        Rochester, New York (group)

1960   "The Photograph as Poetry" at the Pasadena Art Museum,
        Pasadena, California (group)

1961   George Eastman House, Rochester, New York (one-man)

1964   San Francisco Museum of Art (one-man)

1964   Art Institute of Chicago (one-man)

1965   Henry Gallery, University of Washington, Seattle (one-man)

1967   Stanford Art Gallery, Stanford University, Palo Alto, California (one-man)

1968   California College of Arts and Crafts Gallery,
        Oakland, California (one-man)
1968   "North Beach and the Haight-Ashbury" from "Rolling Renaissance"
        Group Show, Focus Gallery, San Francisco (one-man)
1969   Siembab Gallery, Boston, Massachusetts (one-man)
1968–69 "Women, Cameras, and Images I" in the Hall of Photography,
        Museum of History and Technology, Smithsonian Institution,
        Washington, D.C. (one-man)
1969   Phoenix College Library Gallery, Phoenix, Arizona (one-man)
1970   "Platinum Prints," Friends of Photography Gallery,
        Carmel, California (group)

Bibliography

Berding, Christina. "Imogen Cunningham and the Straight Approach," *Modern Photography*, 15 (May 1951), 36–41.

Borden, Elizabeth. "Imogen Cunningham," *U.S. Camera World Annual 1970*, 1969, pp. 60–65, 206, 6 illus.

Craven, George M. "Imogen Cunningham," *aperture*, 11 (1964), 134–74. 45 illus.

Daniel, Edna Tartaul (interviewer). "Imogen Cunningham: Portraits, Ideas, and Design." University of California at Berkeley, Regional Cultural History Project Interview, 1961. 215 typescript pp., illus.

Hall, Norman. "Imogen Cunningham," *Photography* (London), 15 (May 1960), 20–25.

Latour, Ira. "West Coast Photography: Does It Really Exist?" *Photography* (London), 12 (June 1957), 26–45.

Lenz, Herm. "Interview with Three Greats," *U.S. Camera*, 18 (August 1955), 84–87.

M., H. "Imogen Cunningham–Photographer," *Washington Alumnus*, Spring 1965. 8 illus.

Mann, Margery. "Imogen Cunningham," *Infinity*, 15 (November 1966), 25–28. 7 illus.

Maschmedt, Flora Huntley. "Imogen Cunningham—an Appreciation," *Wilson's Photographic Magazine*, 51 (March 1914), 96–99, 113–20. 11 illus.

Newhall, Beaumont. Introduction to *Imogen Cunningham: Photographs 1921–1967*, catalogue of exhibition, Stanford Art Gallery, March 31–April 23, 1967. 25 illus.

White, Minor (ed.). "An Experiment in 'Reading' Photographs," *aperture*, 5 (1957), 66–71. 1 illus.